T0163784

GUERRILLA MARKETING

PUT YOUR ADVERTISING ON STEROIDS!

THIS IS BARELY LEGAL...
BUT YOU CAN STILL
GET AWAY WITH IT!

JAY CONRAD LEVINSON
BEST SELLING AUTHOR WITH OVER 14 MILLION BOOKS SOLD

GUERRILLA MARKETING: PUT YOUR ADVERTISING ON STEROIDS!

By Jay Conrad Levinson

© 2006 Jay Conrad Levinson and Guerrilla Marketing
International. All rights reserved.

No part of this publication may be reproduced or transmitted in any form or
by any means, mechanical or electronic, including photocopying and record-
ing, or by any information storage and retrieval system, without permission in
writing from author or publisher (except by a reviewer, who may quote brief
passages and/or show brief video clips in a review).

Guerrilla Marketing: Put Your Marketing on Steroids! includes and may make
reference to works owned and copyrighted by individuals and/or entities not
affiliated with Jay Conrad Levinson and/or Guerrilla Marketing
International. All such ownership and copyrights remain with their respective
owners. Jay Conrad Levinson and Guerrilla Marketing International make
absolutely no claim of ownership or copyright to any third-party material.

ISBN: 1-933596-13-9   Paperback

ISBN: 1-933596-14-7   e-Book

ISBN: 1-933596-15-5   Audio

Published by:

MORGAN · JAMES
PUBLISHING FOR THE REST OF US...

Morgan James Publishing, LLC

1225 Franklin Ave Ste 325

Garden City, NY 11530-1693

Toll Free 800-485-4943

www.MorganJamesPublishing.com

Cover and Inside Design by:

Heather Kirk

www.GraphicsByHeather.com

Heather@GraphicsByHeather.com

CRITICS ARE RAVING

"Your guerrilla marketing talk was definitely the highlight of our seminar schedule. In fact, many veteran attendees proclaimed you as the best speaker we have presented in our eight-year history."

~ David Scroggy, Director, Comic Book Expo

"A source of inspiration for many independent entrepreneurs."

~ Booklist

"Every book by Jay Levinson is worth reading."

~ Jane Applegate, author of Succeeding in Small Business

"Slam dunk! Without exception, every person who attended our guerrilla marketing seminar said it was well worth their time. Some even commented that they were glad others did not show up because now they have a jump on their competition."

~ Julie Lopresti, Advertising Manager, Pacific Bell

"Ask almost any successful entrepreneur what the best book is for building a small business, and one of Levinson's titles will surely come up."

~ Entrepreneur Business Success Guide

"You gave us concise, practical ideas to implement directly, and virtually all of them were applicable and affordable. Our franchisers are now

committed guerrillas and they will need what is really marketing weapon number one, a book full of more of your terrific ideas. You are, by far, the best and more popular speaker we have ever had and PostalAnnex+ is sure to benefit from your presentation for years to come."

~ David Wilkey, Director of Marketing, PostalAnnex+

"After 'Guerrilla Marketing' became a best-seller, the series took on a life of its own....irrevocably tied in with the unconventional, non-textbook, and practical wisdom of guerrilla business practices for small business."

~ Home Office Computing

"A veritable plum pudding of marketing techniques and secrets."

~ Los Angeles Times

"'Wow!' is the first word that comes to mind when I think of your presentation at Entrepreneur's Day. You really gave our attendees some great advice and tactics to market their businesses more effectively and aggressively."

~ Melissa Anderson, Manager, Public Relations;
The Enterprise Corporation of Pittsburgh

"We can fully appreciate the value of your condensation of marketing techniques into a simple to use format."

~ Jerald N. Cohn, PakMail Centers of America

"Jay did a super job here in Denver. The Guerrilla Marketing Weapons Workshop was a great success, as was his talk at lunch. I heard from many of the attendees that the event was well worth the time and money spent."

~ Joyce Schlose, Manager, The Small Business Profit Center, Greater Denver Chamber of Commerce

"Dear Jay — the recent Business Solutions Forum was a huge success. Key to its success was the high quality of the keynote presentations — these presentations set the bar very high and created the right environment for the AT&T case studies that followed. In fact, one of the keynote presentations remains the subject of a great deal of conversation today. I guess it was simply delivered better and had more real content. It was yours....we thank you!"

~ Macy Jones, Director of Development, Strategic Marketing, Inc.

"Thank you for being part of INTEC's Annual Marketing Meeting last week. Your presentation was outstanding. We heard nothing but positive comments from our members."

~ Dennis C. Hardy, President, INTEC & Company, Inc.

"Thank you for the presentation 'Guerrilla Marketing for Your Small and Growing Business.' Our audience enjoyed it very much. Your contribution to the Quality Learning Series is greatly appreciated."

~ Lisa M. Finley, Marketing Coordinator, U.S. Chamber of Commerce

"Your keynote presentation was terrific. The NBIA Board, staff and audience very much enjoyed your presentation."

~ Dinah Adkins, Executive Director,
National Business Incubation Association

"Your speech at Entrepreneur's Day was great! What a good way to kick-off this conference with such a strong emphasis on marketing. Guerrilla Marketing is just what these entrepreneurs need to understand. Your style and delivery was excellent and I heard many young entrepreneurs talk about the impact it made."

~ John R. Thorne, Chairman, Carnegie Mellon

"We had well over 140 people attend the event and every single one I spoke with was pleased at the value they received and were excited about applying the concepts that you presented to them. You may be interested to know that our chamber will soon be designating its own 'guerrilla marketer' to help promote our services and programs.

~ Ben Buehler-Garcia, Group Vice President,
Tucson Metropolitan Chamber of Commerce

"We have received a great deal of positive feedback and by all standards the Conference was an overwhelming hit — the best one yet! We congratulate you on your outstanding performance that contributed to the Conference's success."

~ Lisa Schaertl and Scott Rothchild,
The Annual Catalog Conference and Exhibition

"Your comments set the stage for a healthy debate about the difficult challenges of achieving future success in an industry historically supported by tremendous asset growth and strong capital markets."

~ Gregory T. Rogers, President, FutureWatch

"The pens and pencils were definitely flying during your presentation of 100 guerrilla marketing tips. Over 85% of survey respondents gave your presentation high ratings. The others, I am sure, simply had a hard time keeping up with your rapid-fire tips, tactics and suggestions."

~ William Annesley, Chief Marketing Officer,
Invisible Fence Company

"The seminar was a huge success. I have received nothing but positive comments about his presentation. We had a great time."

~ Gary Nicholds, Williamson Medical Center

"Your presentation was absolutely fantastic and the feedback has been quite positive."

~ Karlene Johnson, Managing Director, Johnson Communications

The content was great, and I believe that most of our members either heard new material or were given the opportunity to reexamine forgotten concepts. On the whole, I would rate your presentation highly."

~ Eric J. Newman, President, North Bay
Association for Mortgage Brokers

"Your presence certainly helped to make the day a success. Your discussion of guerrilla marketing weapons and methods was pertinent to the issues facing today's business people. Our exit survey results reflected the praise I heard from many of the attendees. The audience reaction to your speech was excellent and many commented on how refreshing it was to receive not only philosophy on how to run a business, but the tools and methods they can implement immediately to see results."

~ Suzanne Clements, Retail Products Manager, The Wichita Eagle

"Marketing whiz wows area CEOs. Jay Levinson, customer analyst and author of widely published books on 'guerrilla marketing,' won over 70 Atlanta-area chief executives Tuesday. He told them how to win over customers."

~ Susan Harte, The Atlanta Journal

"Jay, thank you for your continued contribution to small biz. You are a joy to work with and I couldn't imagine the site without you."

~ Kathleen Doll, Microsoft Small Biz Website Manager

"Jay, as one who has, if not made a living, at least made some money, out of writing, I have the greatest admiration for you, not just for who and what you are, but how cogently you have been able to put your great marketing ideas into such excellently received books."

~ Gerardo Joffe, Author and successful entrepreneur

WE BEGIN WITH A BIO OF JAY CONRAD LEVINSON

Jay Conrad Levinson is the author of the best-selling marketing series in history, "*Guerrilla Marketing*," plus 27 other business books. His guerrilla concepts have influenced marketing so much that today his books appear in 41 languages and are required reading in many MBA programs worldwide.

Jay taught guerrilla marketing for ten years at the extension division of the University of California in Berkeley. And he was a practitioner of it in the United States — as Senior Vice-President at J. Walter Thompson, and in Europe, as Creative Director and Board Member at Leo Burnett Advertising.

He has written a monthly column for *Entrepreneur Magazine*, articles for *Inc. Magazine*, and writes online columns published monthly on the Microsoft Website — in addition to occasional columns in the *San Francisco Examiner*. He also writes online columns regularly for Onvia.com, FreeAgent.com and MarketMakers.com, and InfoUsa.com in addition to occasional columns for Guru.com.

Jay is the Chairman of Guerrilla Marketing International, a marketing partner of Adobe and Apple. He has served on the Microsoft Small Business Council and the 3Com Small Business Advisory Board.

His *Guerrilla Marketing* is a series of books, audio tapes, video-tapes, an award-winning CD-ROM, a newsletter, a consulting organization, an Internet website, and a way for you to spend less, get more, and achieve substantial profits.

TABLE OF CONTENTS

CHAPTER 1

The Guerrilla
Advertising
Strategy

THE GUERRILLA
ADVERTISING STRATEGY

Advertising has changed dramatically since the first ad was run. That advertisement was probably run in a newspaper. Most likely, a farmer told the publisher that he had an extra cow and wanted to sell it. The publisher said, "Hey! I've got a good idea. Let me mention that cow for sale next time I publish my paper." The ad was run. The cow was sold. And advertising started.

It's not quite so simple these days. But two things remain the same. The first is that you need a good idea if you're going to run an ad. Selling that cow was a pretty good idea. The copy probably read: "Cow for sale. $50. Contact Farmer Tom Adams."

You also need an advertising strategy. Farmer Tom Adams' strategy was very simple. Its purpose was to sell one cow. The benefit it offered was a healthy cow at a fair price. The secondary benefit was that a local person was doing the selling. The target audience was other farmers in the community. The action required was to contact Farmer Tom Adams. And the personality of the advertiser was straightforward and no-nonsense.

Armed with that strategy, Farmer Tom sold his cow.

Today, more than two centuries after that first ad was run, you still need a good idea. And you still need a solid advertising strategy. As you can see, such a strategy has only six simple sentences.

Regardless of the complexity of your offering, to give it an infusion of steroids so that it sells what you want it to sell, you must begin with a strategy.

I know you don't sell cows. But let's just suppose that you do sell adventure tours. And suppose the name of your company is Galactic Tours. Here's how you'd craft your strategy:

1. *The first sentence tells the prime purpose of your advertising.*
   "THE PURPOSE OF GALACTIC TOURS ADVERTISING IS TO MOTIVATE PEOPLE TO CALL OR WRITE REQUESTING A FREE VIDEO BROCHURE."

2. *The second sentence spells out the prime benefit you offer.*
   "THE MAIN BENEFIT STRESSED WILL BE THE UNIQUE AND EXCITING DESTINATIONS THAT GALACTIC TOURS' CUSTOMERS CAN VISIT."

3. *The third sentence tells the secondary benefits that you offer.*
   "EMPHASIS WILL ALSO BE PLACED UPON THE CONVENIENCE AND ECONOMY OF GALACTIC TOURS HOLIDAYS AND WELL-TRAINED GUIDES."

4. *The fourth sentence states your target audience or audiences.*
   "OUR TARGET AUDIENCE IS ADVENTUROUS MALES AND FEMALES, BOTH SINGLES AND COUPLES, 21 to 34, WHO HAVE THE FINANCIAL RESOURCES TO AFFORD A GALACTIC TOUR."

5. *The fifth sentence says exactly what you want people to do.*

    "ACTION TO BE TAKEN IS TO MAKE A CALL OR SEND A CARD FOR OUR VIDEO BROCHURE."

6. *The sixth sentence states the personality of your company.*

    "THE PERSONALITY OF GALACTIC TOURS WILL REFLECT INNOVATION, EXCITEMENT AND A WARM, CARING ATTITUDE TOWARDS ALL CUSTOMERS."

Is that all there is to it? Yep. That's all. Procter and Gamble, one of Earth's most sophisticated and successful companies — so successful that 97 percent of homes in America have at least one Procter and Gamble product — uses the same type of simple strategy for all its brands. And most of those brands are either the number one or number two sellers in their category.

True, P&G may have umpteen pages of documentation and details as well, but they begin with a very simple and clear strategy, just like the one you just read.

"Advertising strategy" is merely a fancy phrase that means what **you want and how you'll get it.** If you don't have one, you really have no business advertising in the first place. And it sure won't cost you much to get one.

A brief guerrilla advertising strategy forces you to focus upon the people to whom your advertising is targeted. Always start with the people — then work backwards to the offering. Such a strategy zeros in on the results you want your advertising to achieve, the way you'll obtain those results, and the specific action you want your target audience to take. It provides you with a guide for judging all of your advertising efforts for the next ten or twenty years, or even one hundred years if you go about it right.

The strategy guides you, or the people creating your advertising, without hampering anyone's creativity. It must be expressed in writing, and it should not contain headlines, theme lines or copy. The strategy is totally devoid of specific advertising because it must be solid, yet flexible. Specific words and phrases pin you down. A guerrilla advertising strategy should be developed as your guide and not as your master.

Just like a Procter and Gamble strategy, yours should be deceptively simple when you first read it, but not when you write it. After reading it a couple of times, put it away for 24 hours. It's just too important to be accepted — or rejected — with a hasty snap decision. Look at it with a new consciousness on a different day. See if you still love it and believe it in.

Always remember that your strategy is supposed to generate handsome returns on your advertising investment for the entire century. All future ads, commercials, signs, websites, brochures, and many business decisions will be measured against it.

When is the best time to change that advertising strategy? The week that you first see it, before any advertising has been created according to its dictates, before any money has been spent bringing it to life.

Your approved strategy should be pinned up on the bulletin boards and emblazoned in the minds of everyone who creates advertising for you. Keep it handy in a drawer, on your desktop or in a file so that you can reach for it the moment anyone presents even a tiny shred of advertising to you...or when you have a killer idea yourself.

What if you love, absolutely love the advertising, but it does not fulfill the strategy? Toss it away this very moment. Suppose you hate the advertising, but it does fulfill the strategy. Then give it a second thought. At least it's 50 percent of the way home. Still, you do have every right to love the advertising and for the advertising to fulfill the strategy. The truth is that you have a sacred obligation, as a guerrilla advertiser, to settle for nothing less.

GUERRILLA EXERCISE:

Ask yourself six simple questions:

1. What specific goal do I want my advertising to accomplish?

2. What major benefit do I offer to accomplish that purpose?

3. What other important benefits do I offer to my prospects?

4. Exactly who are those prospects?

5. What action do I want my advertising to motivate?

6. What is my company personality?

GUERRILLA ACTION STEPS:

1. Write an advertising strategy for a current advertiser, based upon the advertising that company has been writing.

2. Write a six-sentence advertising strategy for your own company. Try to do it in 15 minutes, which forces you to focus. It won't take you very long even though it will serve as your guide for years and years.

CHAPTER 2
Targeting Your Audience

TARGETING YOUR AUDIENCE

Now, that you've got a fix on your target audience, you're able to take the next big step and reach them. Of course, that means knowing the most effective ways of finding them. Sometimes it's newspaper. It could be magazines, either consumer or trade publications. Maybe it's the radio. Perhaps it's television. Might the best way be online? How about the yellow pages? And don't forget signs. Guerrillas know that in all likelihood, <u>it's a combination of all of these.</u>

The direct marketing media, such as direct mail, postcard mailings, postcard decks, telemarketing, newsletter, catalogues, infomercials, home shopping shows, the Internet, canvassing, trade shows, and networking functions <u>all work better when combined with advertising, and advertising works best when it's combined with direct marketing.</u>

So don't go off and advertise as soon as you've completed this course. To put that advertising on steroids — to give it added power, first decide which of the direct marketing weapons you will employ to load your advertising guns with live ammo instead of blanks. Advertising without direct marketing makes a lot of noise. But noise doesn't generate profits — or hurt enemies.

Change in advertising has been going on as long as advertising has been going on, and advertising media will continue to change, especially with the Internet becoming so super-powered. The idea for you is to keep your eye on the media so that you are keeping up. I do not advise you to run to the head of the media pack and commit your budget to advertising online. But I do heartily encourage experimentation. Media testing is a guerrilla must.

When selecting media that will hit your target audience right where they live — or work — consider the environment in which your advertising will appear. Pick the media that reach your target audience and will provide the proper environment for the advertising you create: advertising that fits the mood of the readers, listeners, viewers or visitors. It's easier than ever to do this with the highly specialized media now available.

Be sure that you do not fall into the trap of selecting a medium based upon the old-fashioned measurement of "cost per thousand." Instead, base your selection on the criterion of "cost per prospect." Do not fall prey to the statistics quoted by reps of a specific advertising medium. Remember that there are three kinds of lies: dirty, white and statistics.

Advertising legend John Caples said that the two most important factors in advertising are what you say in your ads and where you say it. Where you say it refers to putting your message where it will get into the minds of the largest number of prospects — not people, but prospects — at the lowest cost.

And keep in mind that these days, advertising has a brand new power. It merely has to get people to visit your website. A website is an island. Advertising is a bridge to that island. Large and small businesses online are discovering that truth in a hurry — or else. Advertising is not what it used to be. The Internet has changed its purpose and its strength. Rather than making advertising in the traditional media weaker, the net has made it stronger. That's why all guerrillas must be aware of the new power of advertising.

The first thing to know, and this should come as good news, is that advertising now longer has to make the sale. Not very long ago, advertising's main goal was to make the sale, though there are many other goals. But that has changed dramatically with the growth of dotcom companies all over the Internet. Today, the goal of much advertising is not to make the sale but to <u>direct people to websites</u>.

That does not diminish the power of advertising. Instead, it increases it. With many, if not most, guerrilla-run companies establishing web turf, advertising's newest function is to motivate people to visit a website where they can get far more information than can be delivered by standard media advertising.

Advertising has become the first step in a permission marketing campaign. It invites dialogue and interactivity with prospects and customers by directing people to websites, by offering free brochures, by generating the kind of action that leads to permission to receive marketing messages. Once people grant that permission, which they do at a website or by simply calling to request a brochure — printed or electronic —- that's when serious guerrilla marketing attempts to close the sale.

That means the prime obligation of advertising is to <u>motivate an easy-to-take-action</u>. This should come as good news because it places less of an onus on advertising than ever before. Motivating the action of getting a person to click to your website is a whole lot simpler than motivating a person to part with his or her hard-earned money and risk spending it the wrong way.

Not only is it easier to motivate action, but that action is becoming even easier as being online is now endemic. Over 170 million people are now online, though America Online's chief, Steve Case, pegs the number as being closer to 200 million.

It's not always a whole lot of fun to visit your store or order from your toll-free number, but it is fairly enjoyable to click over to a website and take a gander at what is being offered and how you can benefit. There is a risk when somebody responds to advertising with an order. There is no risk at all if they check your website. Advertising seems to grease the skids to the sale. It takes far less time to learn about you online than to cruise around a mall or drive to a location further away than their computer.

That means advertising can be short, concise, to the point. It no longer has to curry the favor of prospects with long copy, involved graphics or detailed explanations. The Internet can do that for you, allowing you to save on advertising costs. Advertising your website works in all the media — from TV to radio, from magazines to newspaper, from direct mail to billboards. It doesn't take a lot of time or verbiage to get them to spend a few moments checking how your website can improve their lives.

As all guerrillas know, the name of the game in marketing is <u>creating relationships</u>. It's tough to accomplish this with an ad. It's pretty easy with a website, which initiates dialogue by inviting it, by making it as easy as clicking a mouse.

Advertising has always been a method designed to <u>change human behavior</u> by getting people to purchase your product or service. The Internet has changed that. Now, advertising merely has to <u>deflect human behavior</u>, to divert curiosity from an ad or commercial to a website.

There is little question that the online fire burns brightly. There is no question that advertising fuels the online flame.

During the telecast of the Super Bowl played in 1999, I was fairly amazed to see four commercials for dotcom companies. Today, I am even more amazed when I watch a sporting event telecast that does not have a whole gaggle of dotcom commercials.

The big and the small players online are learning from hard experience that they are invisible when they are online. Sure, their site might come up from a search engine or a link from a cooperating company, but the majority of people get their information offline — and that's where guerrillas are marketing their sites. Offline and regularly.

It's true that standard media advertising is interruption marketing, interrupting people in their perusing of the newspaper or magazine, in their viewing of a TV show or listening to the radio. Interruption marketing is crucial, however, as the first step in gaining permission from people to receive your marketing materials. And it is equally crucial in luring them to your website.

Many so-called experts believe that the growth of the Internet signals the demise of advertising. This particular expert believes just the opposite. Advertising now can loom as important as ever, as necessary as ever, and more mandatory for a proper marketing mix than at any time in history.

The larger the Internet grows, the more important the role of advertising and the greater its power. Advertisers must no longer have to move a person from total apathy to purchase readiness with their advertising. Now, all they have to do is move a person from total apathy to mild curiosity. From that point, moving that person to purchase readiness is the job of the website.

GUERRILLA EXERCISE:

1. Put into the writing the demographics of your current customers — their age, gender, income, interests, location and the type of work they do.

2. Ask them by means of a questionnaire what magazines and newspapers they read, which radio stations they listen to, which magazines they read, which websites they access, which trade shows they attend.

3. Tabulate your answers and that will give you a strong direction when it comes to selecting media that will reach them.

GUERRILLA ACTION STEPS:

1. Answer these questions: if you had to select three magazines that reach your target audience, which would you select? If you had to select a section of your daily newspaper in which to advertise, which section would it be?

2. If you had to select three types of radio stations that reach your target audience, which three would you pick? If you had to select three TV shows upon which you would advertise, price being no object, which would you select?

3. Now, look through the magazines and newspapers you selected. Listen to the radio stations you picked. Watch the TV shows you selected. Determine if you'd stay with your original answers.

CHAPTER 3

Selecting Your Advertising Media

SELECTING YOUR
ADVERTISING MEDIA

Okay, you've got a good bead on your target audience, those people who ought to own what you're selling, but for some reason, don't own it yet. Now you've got to determine the most effective way of reaching them and speaking to them.

Sometimes, you can do that with the newspapers. Sometimes, you need magazines — consumer or business. Other times, you'll need radio or television. And don't forget brochures, the yellow pages, signs, and the omnipotent Internet. Here's a major tip: guerrillas realize that most likely, it's a combination of these media.

The direct marketing media such as direct mail, postcard decks, telemarketing, newsletter, catalogues, infomercials, home shopping shows, online marketing, canvassing, trade shows, and networking functions all work much better when they are combined with advertising. And advertising works much better when combined with direct marketing. In a battle, you never have to choose between using a gun or using ammunition. You must use both or you're going to lose that battle.

So don't go off and begin to advertise as soon as you've completed this course. First, decide which of the direct marketing weapons you will employ to load your advertising guns with live ammo instead of blanks. Advertising without direct marketing makes a lot of noise, but doesn't generate profits — or hurt enemies.

When selecting the media that will hit your target audience right where they live — or work — consider the environment in which your advertising will appear. Pick the media that reach that audience and will provide the proper environment for the advertising you will create, advertising that fits the moods of the readers, listeners, viewers or visitors. It's easier to do than ever with the highly specialized media now available.

Some media are apples and others are oranges. What works in one medium may not work in another. <u>Guerrillas have insight into the powers of each medium</u>. They tap those strengths to use the medium to its greatest advantages. Here's what they know about media power:

- **The power of newspapers is news.** Marketing that is newsy gets noticed because news is on the forefront of readers' minds.

- **The power of magazines is credibility.** Readers unconsciously attach to the advertiser the same credibility that they associate with the magazine.

- **The power of radio is intimacy.** Usually radio is a one-on-one situation allowing for a close and intimate connection between listener and marketer.

- **The power of direct mail is urgency.** Time-dated offers that might expire before the recipient can act often motivates them to act now.

- **The power of telemarketing is rapport.** Few media allow you to establish contact in a give-and-take situation as adroitly as the telephone.

- **The power of brochures is the ability to give details.** Few media allow you the time and space to expand on your benefits as much as a brochure.

- **The power of classified ads is information.** Nobody in their right mind actually reads the classified ads except for those in a quest for data.

- **The power of the yellow pages is even more information.** Here, prospects get a line on the entire competitive situation and can compare.

- **The power of television is the ability to demonstrate.** No other media lets you show your product or service in use along with the benefits it offers. TV is still the undisputed heavyweight champ of marketing.

- **The power of the Internet is interactivity.** You can flag a person's attention, inform them, answer their questions and take their orders. You can initiate a dialogue, one of the major advantages the Internet offers.

- **The power of signs is impulse reactions.** Signs motivate people to buy when they are in a buying mood and in a buying arena. Signs either trigger an impulse, or remind people of your other marketing, or both.

■ **The power of flyers is economy.** They can be created, produced and distributed for very little and can even bring about instant results.

■ **The power of billboards is to remind.** They rarely do the whole selling job but they're great at jostling people's memories of your other efforts.

Guerrillas are aware of the specific powers of each medium and design their marketing so as to capitalize upon them. Their awareness gives them more mileage for their marketing investments than if they created marketing while being oblivious to these special strengths. By capitalizing on their insights, they get the very most that each of the media have to offer. Adjusting the message to the medium is an art form and a necessity.

All media were not created equal. Guerrillas are quick to take advantage of these inequalities to increase the effectiveness of each weapon they use.

<u>Remember always that all the media work better if they're supported by the other media</u>. Put your web site onto your TV commercial. Mention your advertising in your direct mail. Refer to your direct mail in your telemarketing. Plant the seeds of your offering with some kinds of marketing and fertilize them with other kinds.

You're not really promoting unless you're cross-promoting. Your trade show booth will be far more valuable to you if you promote it in trade magazines and with flyers put under the doors of hotels near the trade show. Guerrillas try to market their marketing.

Your prospects, being humans, are eclectic people. They pay attention to a lot of media so you can't depend on a mere one medium to motivate a purchase. You've got to introduce a notion, remind people of it, say it again, and then repeat it in different words somewhere else. That share of mind for which guerrilla strive? They get it when they combine several media. They say in their ads, "Call or write for our free brochure."

They say in their Yellow Pages ad, "Get even more details at our website." They enclose a copy of their magazine ad in their mailing. They blow up a copy to use as a sign. Their website features their print ads.

Guerrillas are quick to mention their use of one medium while using another because they realize that people equate broad scale marketing with quality and success. They know that people trust names they've heard of much more than strange and new names; and guerrillas are realistic enough to know that people miss most marketing messages — often intentionally. The remote control is not only a way to save their steps but also a method of eliminating marketing messages.

No matter how glorious their newspaper campaign may be, guerrillas realize that not all of their prospects read the paper so they've got to get to these people in another way. No matter how dazzling their website, it's like a grain of sand in a desert if it is not pointed out to an unknowing and basically uncaring public.

Cross-promoting in the media is another way to accomplish the all-important task of repetition. One way to repeat yourself and implant your message is to say it over and over again. Another way is to say it in several different places. Guerrillas try to do both. Nothing is left to chance. If you saw a yellow pages ad that made you an offer from a company you've never heard of and another with the same offer except that the ad said, "As advertised on television," you'd probably opt for the second because of that added smidgen of credibility. Credibility creates confidence and confidence creates sales.

GUERRILLA EXERCISE:

1. Study the media that you've selected at the end of Lesson Two to see if any of your competitors are also advertising there. If they are, consider that to be a good sign.

2. Go the library and look at the Standard Rate & Data Directories. Those will give you the costs and circulation figures for the media that make most sense to you. Call and ask for media kits for the media you're most likely to use.

GUERRILLA ACTION STEPS:

1. Make a list of the products and services that you've purchased as a result of advertising. Try to determine exactly what motivated you to make your selections.

2. Be very honest with yourself while assessing advertising directed at you for one full week. Ask yourself if you're fascinated more with the advertising or the offering being advertised. Ask yourself if the advertising moved you one bit closer to becoming a customer. You'll find that very little advertising is really making a cogent point to you. The meaning is that the competition is asleep at the wheel. When you put your advertising on steroids, you'll be switching to a much higher gear.

CHAPTER 4

Planning Your Campaign

PLANNING YOUR CAMPAIGN

Talk about momentum! You've got an advertising strategy. You know who your best prospects are. You have a good idea of exactly how to reach them. Your advertising is going to be teeming with strength and power as you continue to go through the process of infusing it with steroids. These steroids aren't going to wear away, aren't going to disappear, and aren't going to be a temporary fix. The steps you're taking now will forever energize your advertising. And that means boost your profits.

Okay, what now? What are you going to say to your prospects? What you say and when you say it are essential decisions for your success. We're all aware of some companies that are saying all the right things to the wrong people and others that are saying all the wrong things to the right people.

You want to say the right things to the right people at the right time and in the right way. Determining how to pull that off means leaning upon your advertising strategy. It's your roadmap. You don't have to make things up as you go along because you know the direction toward which you should be heading. It's stated in the first sentence of your strategy.

That strategy also keeps you aware of the realities of your budget and helps you say things that will be as beneficial in the future as they will be in the present moment. The better you know the real truth about your prospects and customers, the better equipped you'll be to say exactly what will motivate them to make purchases from you. Here's a down-and-dirty examination of them:

You may think you know why your customers buy from you, but there's a good chance they buy for reasons other than the reasons you think. Or they don't buy for reasons that may escape you.

People seek a wide array of benefits when they're in a buying mindset. If you are communicating any one of those benefits to the people who want them this very instant, you've virtually made the sale. People do not buy because advertising is clever, but because it strikes a responsive chord in their mind, and its resonance makes that person want the advantages of what you are selling.

Your customers do not buy because they're being advertised to or sold to. Instead, they buy because you help them realize the merits of owning what you offer.

They often buy because you offer them instant gratification — such as I sought when El Niño flexed his muscles and my roof began to leak. Sprinting to the yellow pages, I called the one roof repair company that offered emergency service, for there I was, smack dab in the middle of an emergency.

It was an easy decision for me. The company offered just the benefit I needed. I was in the market for a specific benefit and there it was, grinning up at me from the directory. If the company's ad heralded their new roofing materials, I would have ignored it.

Like most people, I was looking to buy a benefit, not a feature. Everybody knows that. But the truth is that people don't always buy benefits. They buy a whole lot more:

- They buy promises you make. So make them with care.

- They buy the promises they want personally fulfilled.

- They buy your credibility or don't buy if you lack it.

- They buy solutions to their problems.

- They buy you, your employees, your service department.

- They buy wealth, safety, success, security, love and acceptance.

- They buy your guarantee, reputation and good name.

- They buy other people's opinions of your business.

- They buy expectations based upon your marketing.

- They buy believable claims, not simply honest claims.

- They buy hope for their own and their company's future.

- They buy brand names over strange names.

- They buy the consistency they've seen you exhibit.

- They buy the stature of the media in which you market.

- They buy the professionalism of your marketing materials.

- They buy value, which is not the same as price.

- They buy selection and often the best of your selection.

- They buy freedom from risk, granted by your warranty.

- They buy acceptance by others of your goods or services.

- They buy certainty.

- They buy convenience in buying, paying and lots more.

- They buy respect for their own ideas and personality.

- They buy your identity as conveyed by your marketing.

- They buy style — just the kind that fits their own style.

- They buy neatness and assume that's how you do business.

- They buy easy access to information about you, offered by your website.

- They buy honesty, for one dishonest word means no sale.

- They buy comfort, offerings that fit their comfort zone.

- They buy success; your success can fit with theirs.

- They buy good taste and know it from bad taste.

- They buy instant gratification and don't love to wait.

- They buy the confidence you display in your own business.

It's also important to know what customers do not buy: fancy adjectives, exaggerated claims, clever headlines, special effects, marketing that screams, marketing that even hints at amateurishness, the lowest price anything (though 14 percent do), unproven items, or gorgeous graphics that get in the way of the message.

They also do not buy humor that hides benefits, offerings heralded with unreadable type, poor grammar, misspelled words, salespeople who don't listen, or things they don't fully understand or trust.

The best advertising of all involves prospects and informs customers. It builds confidence and invites a purchase. Best and most unique of all — it gets through to people. That's why knowing the truth about them will help you to stand apart from your competitors and shine in the minds of your prospects and customers.

Guerrillas know that an advertising campaign must have continuity to do the persuading job well. In advertising, intermittent communication is no communication at all. Your plan must have consistency built right into it. The idea is not merely to flirt with your public, but to convince them. There is a huge difference between the two. Any true advertising expert will tell you that frequency and persistence are the secrets of success in advertising. A major commitment to one or a few of the media will work better in most cases than an across-the-board plan with a variety of media but a short insertion schedule.

Plan your campaign so that you are consistent, but never boring, committed, but never predictable. You've got to build special promotions into your plan to keep your staff on their feet and your competition off balance. The only part of the plan that is engraved in stone is your identity. Flexibility and an ability to make alterations in your advertising are crucial.

All guerrillas know that when it comes to creating advertising, there are three factors to consider: speed, quality, and economy. They also know that they get to select any two of these factors. You can bet they opt for quality and economy every time. Their careful planning eliminates the need for speed.

When you begin to craft the messages you will convey, keep this depressing information in mind:

1. The first time a man looks at an advertisement, he does not see it.

2. The second time, he does not notice it.

3. The third time, he is conscious of its existence.

4. The fourth time, he faintly remembers having seen it before.

5. The fifth time, he reads it.

6. The sixth time, he turns up his nose at it.

7. The seventh time, he reads it through and says, "Oh brother!"

8. The eighth time, he says, "Here's that confounded thing again!"

9. The ninth time, he wonders if it amounts to anything.

10. The tenth time, he asks his neighbor if he has tried it.

11. The eleventh time, he wonders how the advertiser makes it pay.

12. The twelfth time, he thinks it must be a good thing.

13. The thirteenth time, he thinks perhaps it might be worth something.

14. The fourteenth time, he remembers wanting such a thing a long time.

15. The fifteenth time, he is tantalized because he cannot afford to buy it.

16. The sixteenth time, he thinks he will buy it some day.

17. The seventeenth time, he makes a memorandum to buy it.

18. The eighteenth time, he swears at his poverty.

19. The nineteenth time, he counts his money carefully.

20. The twentieth time he sees the ad, he buys what it is offering.

The list you've just read was written by Thomas Smith of London in 1885. But here we are moving bravely ahead in the 2000s, so how much of that list is valid right now, today? The answer is all of it.

Guerrillas know that the single most important element of superb marketing is commitment to a focused plan. Do you think commitment is easy to maintain after an ad has run nineteen times and nobody is buying? It's not easy. But marketing guerrillas have the coolness to hang in there because they know how to get into a prospect's unconsciousness, where most purchase decisions are made. They know it takes repetition. This knowledge fuels their commitment. Anyhow, they never thought it was going to be easy.

As real estate is location location location, advertising is frequency frequency frequency.

GUERRILLA EXERCISE:

Whether you'll be advertising on the radio, on television, on the Internet or in print, practice saying what you have to say by putting it on paper, in the following order:

1. Create a headline

2. Create a subhead

3. Do a rough sketch of the graphics

4. Write a caption for each photo or illustration

5. Edit what you've written up to this point

Now you have the framework for a real advertisement.

GUERRILLA ACTION STEPS:

1. Write a full-page magazine ad for one of the magazines you've selected, determining the graphics, then writing copy that uses several of these magic words in advertising:

FREE	LOVE	SAFE	NEW
BENEFITS	RIGHT	YOU	GUARANTEED
SECURITY	SALE	NOW	WINNINGS
VALUE	ONLINE	FUN	SAVE
GAIN	MONEY	HAPPY	ADVICE
HOW TO	WANTED	YOUR	SECRET

EASY	PROVEN	SUDDENLY	DISCOVERY
PROUD	PEOPLE	HEALTHY	RICHES
NATURAL	FAST	PRECIOUS	WEALTHY
SOLUTION	MAGIC	WHY	COMFORT

2. Be certain not to use any of these tragic words in advertising:

BUY	DIFFICULT	DEATH	OBLIGATION
WRONG	ORDER	FAILURE	DECISION
FAIL	BAD	DEAL	COST
SELL	LIABILITY	WORRY	LOSS
HARD	DETAILS	CONTRACT	

CHAPTER 5
Writing Headlines That Persuade

WRITING HEADLINES THAT PERSUADE

Advertising is persuasion at its core. You must persuade individuals or groups to part with one of their most prized possessions: Their money.

All guerrillas know that advertising is a fancy word that means selling, and selling is a fancy word that means persuasion. If you can't persuade, you can't sell. If you can't sell, you can't advertise successfully. Persuasion is a crucial ingredient in the steroids cocktail if you have a business and a fondness for the things that money can buy.

Many people who think they can't succeed at advertising because they can't persuade seem to do a dandy job of persuading their spouses to be on time, their kids to do their homework, and their associates to accept the idea they've just put on the table. The moral: there are a lot of closet persuaders out there.

Guerrillas rev up their powers of persuasion with two kinds of insight: insight into their prospects and customers combined with insight into their own product or service. Without those insights, you're a dead duck. With them, you're a guerrilla, poised for victory and profitability.

You have already focused upon who to persuade. That may be the toughest question your business must answer. The right answer can lead to the attainment of your wildest dreams, and you don't have to tell me how wild those dreams are. When you know who to persuade, you are only part of the way home. You must also know what is important to them.

Here's a flash: persuasion can be straight-forward. Most business owners, and even those who create advertising for them, think that persuading has a lot to do with pussyfooting around and playing needless games. To begin with, they haven't a clue as to the exact person they should be persuading. If they ever find out, they don't know the hot buttons that ignite that person.

No wonder they're pussyfooting! There's not a lot to be candid about. I'm the first to admit that not every persuasion attempt you make will work out the way you want. But I'm here in the pages of this book to remind you to realize why some attempts succeed, to realize why some fail, and to realize the difference between the two.

Within that difference resides your power of persuasion. If you become a better persuader, you become a better salesperson. If you become a better salesperson, you become a better advertiser. You become a guerrilla — one who achieves conventional goals with unconventional methods.

Guerrillas ask themselves questions after successful persuasions. "What was the critical insight that I used?" "How did I use it?" Of failures, they ask: "What insight should I have seen?" "How did my attempt miss it?" Frequently, failures are caused by persuaders failing to understand the person being persuaded. The deeper you amble into the head of your prospect, the more persuasive you will become because of the scope of your understanding.

The meaning of guerrilla persuasion: knowing your customers and prospects so well that it's a cinch to connect their goals with yours.

So now you know the truth. There is no magic in persuasion. There is simply research time and your own energy. Back in the 1900's, ad great Claude Hopkins said, and I hope you'll excuse his sexism, "The advertising man studies the consumer. He tries to place himself in the position of the buyer. His success largely depends on doing that to the exclusion of everything else." The keys to persuasion are in shoes and eyes. Walk a mile in your customer's shoes and see things through his eyes.

After all, you can't learn to be a first-rate bullfighter unless you've first learned to be a bull. Guerrilla persuading means connecting with consumers on the level of the mind. The connection begins in your own mind — and it continues until a sale is made. Gentle persuasion can be as powerful as pressured persuasion. Slow motion persuasion works better than high speed persuasion. And all persuasion begins with connection.

Headlines are used in ads, commercials, telemarketing calls, direct mail letters, websites, sales presentations and more. Can you write great ones? You know the magic words and the tragic words, but can you really write a headline that persuades people to either:

buy your offering, read your copy, visit your website, or call your toll-free phone number? It's not easy. But you'll know how right after you read this lesson.

Every guerrilla destined for advertising victories knows very well that if you have ten hours to spend creating an advertisement, you should spend nine of them creating the headline. It's the first impression you make, often the only impression, and the rest of your advertising will live or die by the quality of that headline.

Don't think that just because you don't run print ads your headline is not important. Another way of thinking about a headline to think of it as the first thing you say to prospects. Wise marketing people have said that you should picture yourself knocking on someone's door which is then opened by a very busy person. You can say one thing before that person slams the door in your face or opens it widely and invites you in.

You have the opportunity to tell your whole story in one line or to say something so intriguing that the prospect will want to hear more. You'll have this opportunity in print ads to be sure, but also with first lines of TV spots and radio commercials, with opening lines of letters and postcards, with first statements made by sales reps or telemarketers, in brochures and on websites, in yellow pages ads and sales videos, in classified ads and infomercials, at trade shows and catalogs. People will decide to read or hear your message or to ignore you completely. It all depends on your headline. If your headline is a loser, you have three strikes against you when you step up to the plate. Lotsa luck!

All guerrillas on earth are delighted that technology now makes marketing easier than ever, that websites enable them to market with even more fervor, and that new software lets them create dynamite marketing materials right in their own offices — but they never lose sight of the fundamentals, and headlines are the cornerstone. It's the headline that dictates your positioning in your prospects' minds and it's the headline that will attract either attention or apathy. Nothing you say to a prospect is more important.

In print, you have one line to get that attention. On radio or TV, you have three seconds, and you have those same three seconds with any sales presentations or telemarketing calls. Win attention and interest during that brief period or you won't win it later. There will be no later.

Now that I've alerted you as to the importance of headlines, here are 20 hints to help you create winning ones:

1. Know that your headline must either convey an idea or intrigue the reader or listener into wanting to learn more.

2. Speak directly to the reader or listener, one at a time, even if 20 million people will be exposed to your message.

3. Write your headline in newsy style.

4. Use words that have the feeling of an important announcement.

5. Test headlines that start with the word "announcing."

6. Test headlines that use the word "new."

7. Put a date in your headline.

8. Feature your price, if you're proud of it, in your headline.

9. Feature your very easy payment plan.

10. Announce a free offer and use the word "free."

11. Offer information of value right in your headline.

12. Start to tell a fascinating story; guerrillas know that marketing really is the truth made fascinating.

13. Begin your headline with the words, "How to."

14. Begin your headline with "why," "which," "you," "this" or "advice."

15. Use a testimonial style headline.

16. Offer the reader a test.

17. Use a huge one-word headline.

18. Warn the reader not to delay buying.

19. Address your headline to a specific person; every day there are specific individuals who want exactly what you are offering.

20. Set your headline in the largest type on the page and start your verbal presentations right with the headline.

If the reader or listener isn't stopped by your headline, they'll move onto something else that does stop them. After all, they're looking to be stopped by something and if it's not your message it will be someone else's. Headlines and opening lines are your initial bonds to your prospects. And never forget for one second that what you say is the manner in which you say it. Bend over backwards to be believed.

Boring and indirect headlines sabotage thoughtful copy and brilliant graphics every day of the year, including Christmas. Stupendous offers are not accepted by a ready public because the headline or opening line fell down on the job. There are far more terrible headlines than great ones in every edition of every newspaper and magazine.

In such an atmosphere, guerrillas thrive. They love when others run headlines that are cutsie pie and off the point. They are enthralled when competitors run ads that draw attention away from the prime offering because a copywriter wanted to make a pun or get a laugh. But you can be sure their own headlines always get noticed, generate readership, attract responses, and result in profits.

Although a company cannot achieve greatness solely based upon their headlines and opening lines, without solid first impressions, its growth will be seriously impeded. Your job may be to create headlines or to judge them. It is one of your most important tasks.

If you can persuade and you can put persuasion into your headlines, you're a pharmacologist when it comes to putting your advertising on steroids.

GUERRILLA EXERCISE:

1. Look through any magazine and newspaper and rewrite five of the headlines — making them more persuasive.

2. Listen to the opening lines of several television commercials and rewrite five of the lines — making them more persuasive.

3. Visit a selection of websites and rewrite their headlines — making them more persuasive.

GUERRILLA ACTION STEPS:

1. Create three superbly persuasive headlines for a print or newspaper ad you might run for your own business.

2. Create three supremely persuasive opening lines you might use in a radio or television commercial for your own business.

3. Create three powerfully persuasive headlines you might use on the home page of your website.

CHAPTER 6

The Power Of A Competitive Advantage

THE POWER OF A COMPETITIVE ADVANTAGE

Everybody offers benefits in their advertising, but guerrillas stress those benefits that only they offer. That's where to hang your advertising hat.

Many of today's products and services are so similar to each other that the only difference is in their advertising. They try to woo new customers with jingles, special effects, gimmicks, freebies, sales and fancy production. These advertising devices are the final refuge of people with limited imaginations. Although there is little question that they can help, a serious guerrilla knows there are other ways to advertise with far more potency.

The most important of these are competitive advantages. If your widget doubles a company's profits, grows hair on bald heads, or attracts life-long partners, you don't have to stoop to using gimmicks. Jingles will just get in the way of clarity. Just the truth will do very nicely, thank you.

Perhaps you have a plethora of competitive advantages. The only ones that can be translated into instant profits for your company are the marketable ones. A new kind of fabricating material, unless it is a dramatic advancement with dazzling benefits, will probably only bore your prospects.

The idea is to identify your marketable competitive advantages, then concentrate heavily upon those. If you don't have any marketable competitive advantages, realize that a savvy guerrilla discovers them or creates them.

The area most fertile for creating a new competitive advantage is service. There are gobs of automobile detailers in my area. All of them charge about the same price, do about the same job. But why did I pick P&H Class Details to detail my car? Because they make house calls. I didn't have to waste one second of my precious time attending to the details of detailing. Instead, I made a phone call and P&H took over from there.

I was impressed by their competitive advantage — though they didn't even mention that advantage when they started in business. Reason: they didn't offer it then. But they surveyed the competitive scene, then invented it and advertised it. That's exactly what I'm recommending to you.

See what your competitors are offering. Patronize them if you can. Keep an eagle eye for areas in which you can surpass them, especially in service. Perhaps you can offer faster delivery, on-site service, gift wrapping, more frequent follow-up, maintenance for a period of time, installation, a longer guarantee, training, shipping, the possibilities are virtually endless.

A customer questionnaire will turn up many nifty areas upon which you may concentrate. Ask why people patronize the businesses they do. Ask what the ideal business would offer. Ask what they like best about your company. Pay close attention to the answers because some might be pointing directly at the competitive advantages you might want to offer.

Does it cost much to offer a competitive advantage? Nope. It takes brainpower, time, energy and imagination, but it is not a matter of money. And it is precisely why guerrillas score so many bull's-eyes — using the brute force of a brilliant competitive edge to negate the need for a huge budget.

It may be that you already have a competitive advantage that is not yet advertised as such. Back in the thirties, a copywriter went for a tour of the Lucky Strike cigarette factory. When he came across a large warm room filled with tobacco, he asked the person giving the tour what that was all about. "Oh, that's our toasting room," said the tour leader. "Do all cigarette companies have toasting rooms?" asked the canny copywriter. "Sure, they all do," was the answer.

But nobody else was advertising them. The writer suggested that Luckies say "It's toasted!" right on the front of the package. The advertising director complied and soon, the brand became America's number one seller — emphasizing a competitive advantage not recognized as such by their competition.

Such stories are legion. The important thing for you to do is to identify or create your own, and then let it propel you to victory.

To begin to find your competitive advantage, make a list of the benefits you offer. Of those benefits, many are being offered by your competition as well. But which do you offer and they do not offer? Those are your edges. Which of those are most important to your prospects? Once you have identified those competitive advantages, you've got a ticket to ride — all the way to the bank.

When searching for your competitive advantage, focus on the problems that besiege your prospect. Guerrillas know that it's easier to sell the solution to a problem than to sell a positive benefit. That's why they position themselves as problem-solvers.

A well-known axiom of advertising has always been that it is much simpler to sell the solution to a problem than it is to sell a positive benefit. For this reason, guerrillas position their companies to be ace problem-solvers. They home in on the problems confronting their prospects, and then offer their products or services as solutions to the problems.

Almost all companies are beset with problems of one sort or another. Your job, as a right-thinking guerrilla, is to spot those problems. One of the ways to do this is through networking. Networking is not a time to toot your own trombone, but to ask questions, listen carefully to the answers, and keep your advertising radar attuned to the presence of problems. After learning them, you can contact the prospect and talk about the prospect's problems and your solutions to those nasty dilemmas.

You can also learn of problems that require solving at trade shows, professional association meetings, prospect question-naires, and even sales calls. As you already know, people do not buy shampoo; they buy clean, great-looking hair. That means selling a benefit. A way that some shampoos have achieved prof-its is by reassuring people that the shampoo cleans hair, then stressing that it solves the problem of unmanageable hair — a benefit and a solution to a problem.

Right now, products and services that are enjoying success are those that help people quit smoking, lose weight, earn more money, improve health, grow hair, eliminate wrinkles, and save time. These are problem-solving products and services.

You can be sure that some of these can also be positioned as offerings that accentuate a positive, but savvy company presi-dents saw to it that their offerings were positioned as things that could eliminate a negative.

Your biggest job is to be sure your products and services do the same. Perhaps you'll have to undergo a major repositioning. That's not bad if it improves your profits. Far more doors will be open to you if you can achieve it.

Maybe you know right off what the major problems are facing your prospects. Your marketing should highlight these problems. Then, it should offer your product or service as the ideal solution.

If you don't know the problems, knock yourself out learning them. Regardless of the benefits you offer, realize that their importance is generally overshadowed by the problems confronting a prospect.

It's really not that difficult to position your offering as a problem-solver. But once you do, you'll find that the task of advertising becomes a whole lot easier in a hurry. You'll have to examine your offerings in the light of how they affect your prospects. So what if they are state-of-the-art? That pales in comparison with their ability to reduce your prospect's overhead. So what if they are lower in price than they used to be? That's nothing compared with their ability to help your prospects combat loneliness.

Those prospects care about saving money, to be sure. But they care far more about feeling alone and unloved. If you can solve that problem for your prospects, buying what you sell will be very easy for them. Prospects don't really care about your company; they care about their problems. If you can solve them, then prospects will care a great deal about your company, and they'll want to buy what you are selling.

Amazingly, even though this all makes sense, many companies are unaware of the importance of problem-solving. They're so wrapped up in the glories of their product or service that they are oblivious to how well it solves problems. So they sell features and neglect benefits. They sell the obtaining of positives instead of the eliminating of negatives.

Keep the concept of problem-solving alive in: your mind, your advertising, your sales presentations, and your competitive advantage. Be sure your employees are tuned into the same wave length. Once this happens, I have a feeling that you're going to be one happy guerrilla.

GUERRILLA EXERCISE:

1. Make a list of all the benefits that you offer.

2. Put a circle around those benefits which are also competitive advantages.

3. Study the advertising of your competitors to determine what they consider to be their competitive advantages.

GUERRILLA ACTION STEPS:

1. Make a list of the problems faced by your prospects.

2. Make a list of the solutions you offer to solve those problems.

3. Create a headline stating the problem and a subhead offering your product or service as a solution.

CHAPTER 7

Wonderful And Horrible Advertising

WONDERFUL AND HORRIBLE ADVERTISING

Because more marketing funds are invested in advertising than in any other weapon of guerrilla marketing, and because an embarrassingly huge amount of that investment is just plain wasted, marketing guerrillas know home truths about copy, graphics, what makes commercials good or bad, and why so much advertising fails.

Guerrillas know ten things that advertising copy should always be:

1. Readable

2. Informative

3. Clear

4. Honest

5. Simple

6. On strategy

7. Motivating

8. Competitive

9. Specific

10. Believable

They know ten things not to do with advertising graphics:

1. Don't let the art overpower the idea.

2. Don't let the art overpower the headline.

3. Don't let the art overpower the copy.

4. Don't let the art fail to advance the sale.

5. Don't let the art fail to grab casual readers or viewers.

6. Don't let the art fail to get the ad or spot noticed.

7. Don't let the art fail to be different.

8. Don't let the art be created in a hurry.

9. Don't let the art fight the product's identity.

10. Don't let the art dominate the ad.

Guerrillas know what makes a TV commercial a total loser:

1. It is more entertaining than motivating.

2. It is not clear with its promise.

3. It is not visual, but depends on words.

4. It is schlocky, lacking in credibility.

5. It is high-pressure or exaggerative.

6. It is a fabulous film but a terrible commercial.

7. It is so clever you forget who ran it.

8. It is so wrapped up in special effects; it's devoid of an idea.

9. It is too complex for an idea to come shining through.

10. It is boring, boring, boring.

Guerrillas also know what makes a TV commercial a winner:

1. It is clear about its competitive advantage.

2. It is intensely visual.

3. It is professional looking.

4. It is believable and credible.

5. It creates a powerful desire.

6. It is focused on advancing the sale, not being clever.

7. It is wrapped up with the product.

8. It demonstrates the benefit.

9. It is fascinating even the tenth time you see it.

Guerrillas are fascinated by the failures of advertising and know the main reasons why so much of it falls short:

1. Premature abandonment.

2. Silly positioning.

3. Failure to focus.

4. Starting without a plan.

5. Picking the wrong media for the right audience.

6. Picking the right media for the wrong audience.

7. Being unclear to prospects.

8. Not understanding customers.

9. Not understanding self.

10. Exaggeration that undermines truth.

11. Not keeping up with change.

12. Unrealistic expectations.

13. Overspending or underspending.

14. Saving money in the wrong places.

15. Inattention to tiny, but nuclear-powered details.

16. Missing the point about profitability.

17. Thinking it can be done without hard work.

18. Unimpressive first impressions.

19. Committees and layers of management.

20. Not using media to their greatest advantage.

21. Not supporting advertising with other marketing.

22. Starting out in the wrong direction.

23. Allowing success to beget lethargy.

24. Judging the future by the past.

25. Boring advertising.

What Guerrillas know about creativity in advertising:

1. The best measure of creativity is profitability.

2. Remember that creativity begins with an idea.

3. The idea is found within the product or service.

4. The idea will write its own advertisements.

5. Creativity doesn't care where it comes from.

6. The best creativity spawns ideas with long lives.

7. Think of advertising as the truth made fascinating.

8. The more specific you are the more creative you can be.

9. Creativity does not come from inspiration.

10. Creativity comes from knowledge.

Seek knowledge in 10 Areas to put your advertising on steroids:

1. Customers

2. Prospects

3. Competitors

4. Equivalent businesses elsewhere

5. Your own industry

6. Current events

7. Economic trends

8. Your own offering

9. Your community

10. Successful advertising

Ten Advertising Ideas With Longevity

1. Maytag's lonely repairman

2. StarKist's Charlie the Tuna

3. Pillsbury's Doughboy

4. Allstate's good hands

5. United's friendly skies

6. Green Giant's ho ho ho

7. Merrill Lynch's bull

8. The Dreyfus Fund's Lion

9. Marlboro's cowboy

10. Energizer's bunny

Five steps to being creative:

1. Find your inner amazement — it's in every product and service.

2. Select your competitive edge — it will infuse your advertising with a high-powered dosage of steroids.

3. Break the advertising barrier with believability.

4. Get your audience to sit up and take notice.

5. Tell them exactly what to do next.

Advertising is really quite simple — unless you make it complicated, unless you think it is something it is not, unless you fail to factor reality into your creativity.

When your advertising is on steroids, it will be such a profit-producer for you that it will seem as though your profits are also on steroids.

GUERRILLA EXERCISE:

1. Examine the media in your area — radio, television, magazines and newspapers, and then make a list of five examples of wonderful advertising and five examples of horrible advertising. Your increased awareness of current advertising will help yours become more effective.

2. Go online to find five home pages that are examples of wonderful advertising and five more that are horrible examples of advertising.

3. Browse your yellow pages directory and make a list of five ads that attracted your attention to the company. What can you learn from each of those ads?

GUERRILLA ACTION STEPS:

1. Select a print advertisement for a business in the same industry as yours. Rewrite the ad to make it stronger in as many areas as you can. Be sure the ad continues to be for the same business that ran it, but realize what the rewriting has taught you.

2 Create a sixty-second radio commercial for your business, forcing you to rely upon words, sounds and music instead of visuals. Although people obtain 80 percent of what they know by visual means, you can't

ignore that other 20 percent. And you can learn to conjure visual images with words merely by putting your commercial in writing. A sixty-second radio commercial has about 150 words. Write the commercial to sell your offering as though your business depended upon this single commercial. In real life, repetition will be your greatest ally, but for this action step, go directly for the jugular.

CHAPTER 8

How To Put Your Credibility On Steroids

HOW TO PUT YOUR CREDIBILITY ON STEROIDS

Every guerrilla knows that the number one factor influencing purchase decisions is confidence. The road to confidence is paved with credibility. Advertising won't pave that road unless you do it right. Here's where you learn to do it profitably.

Having the lowest price won't help you much if your prospect doesn't trust you in the first place. Offering the widest selection and the most convenience won't aid your cause if your prospect thinks you're a crook.

You've got to face up to the glaring reality that prospects won't call your toll-free number, access your website, mail your coupon, come into your store, visit your trade show booth, talk to your sales rep, talk to you on the phone, or even accept your generous freebie if they aren't confident in your company.

Time zips on by. Some of your prospects are now doing business with your competitors. Those prospects can't afford to waste it or their money with companies that haven't earned their confidence. In order to earn that confidence — no stroll in the park, as you've most likely learned — you've got to use guerrilla advertising as well as specific guerrilla marketing weapons and use them properly. I emphasize "properly" because even a smart bomb isn't a valuable weapon if it lands on your foot.

Guerrillas think in terms of getting down to the business of achieving and deserving credibility. In their advertising and all their other marketing materials, whatever they say or show with their main message, also carries a "meta-message" — an unstated, yet powerful communiqué to prospects.

A large, handsome ad in a respected publication carries a much more potent meta-message than a small, crude-looking ad in a free newspaper. And keep in mind that meta-messages are conveyed by more than just advertising. The meta-message for Deuce Cleaners of a superbly written direct mail letter on very inexpensive stationery is going to be quite different from the meta-message of the same letter for Ace Cleaners on costly stationery that looks and feels exquisite.

The paper stock carries a strong meta-message. So does the real or metered stamp. The typeface speaks volumes and the printed — or handwritten — signature is even more eloquent. The Ace Cleaners letter has superb stock, a clear and elegant typeface and a hand-signed signature, using blue ink and a fountain pen. These are tiny details. Tiny, but nuclear-powered.

Not surprisingly, the Deuce Cleaners letter, even though worded exactly like the Ace Cleaners letter, will not draw as healthy a response because of its weak meta-message. A powerful meta-message inspires confidence.

Entire advertising plans fall by the wayside because inattention to seemingly unimportant details undermines the prospect's confidence — even if that confidence was earned elsewhere.

An amateurish logo makes your company seem like an amateur. Any hint of amateurism in your marketing indicates to your prospects <u>the potential for amateurism</u> elsewhere in your company — maybe even throughout your company. Does this mean that small ads, a plain Jane website, fuzzy type, and poor English destroy your credibility? Not entirely. But shabbiness in these areas certainly does not contribute to your credibility.

<u>Absolutely everything you do that is called marketing influences your credibility</u>. The influence will be positive or negative, depending upon your taste, intelligence, sensitivity, and awareness of this power.

Be aware of it the moment you start operating your business, and if not then, right now. Begin the quest with the name of your company, your logo, your theme line, location, stationery, business card, package, brochure, business forms, interior decor, website, fusion marketing partners, even the attire worn by you and your people. Convey that credibility to the largest number of people with your advertising. All those other factors can play an important part in your success. But advertising will play the part to a much larger audience.

Team up with your advertising to communicate even more credibility with the building you're in, the people you employ, the technology you use, the follow-up in which you engage, the attention you pay to customers, the testimonials you display, your trade show booth, your signs, and surely the neatness of your premises.

The way your phones are answered can gain or lose credibility for you. Just yesterday, I decided not to make an expensive purchase from a store I had called simply because they put me on telephone hold for too long. Minor detail? Maybe, but somebody else now has my deposit check.

You gain credibility with your advertisements, listings in directories, columns and articles you write, and the talks you give. You gain it with your newsletter. You gain even more by your support of a noble cause such as the environment. All these little things add up to something called <u>your reputation</u>.

The most important word in advertising — <u>commitment</u> — is something that also fuels your credibility. When people see that you are maintaining consistency in your advertising, they'll assume you're just as committed to quality and service.

All of your weapons must communicate the same meta-message — one that fits in with everything else in your advertising and with the reality of your offerings. You don't need a Lincoln Continental identity to succeed with a bait shop.

Credibility is not automatic but it is do-able. Give a seminar. Work hard for a community organization. Nudge customers into referring your business. Word-of-mouth is omnipotent in the credibility quest. The idea is for you to establish your expertise, your authority, your integrity, your conscientiousness, your professionalism, and therefore — your credibility. The more you have, the better your advertising will work. The better your advertising works, the more credibility you'll have. It's a merry-go-round ride you're gonna love.

When that PR person gets you into the newspaper, make reprints of the article and frame them, include them on your website, into your brochure, pop them into your newsletter, put them on your counter, stick them in your store window — and for sure, show them in your ads. Cost? A bit of time. Result? A lot of credibility.

Trade shows can enhance your credibility and so can free demonstrations. Free consultations can do wonders for it and so can free samples. Do glitz and glamour enhance your credibility? They do —- but be careful that you don't send out the wrong message. If you're a discounter, glitz can sabotage your identity.

Wanna shortcut to credibility? Run a full-page ad in a regional edition of a national magazine. Just running the ad won't net much credibility for you, but the reprints you display, mail, incorporate into other marketing, and proudly disseminate will. They'll all proclaim "As advertised in Time magazine." And if they don't say, Time, they'll say some other prestigious publication.

All the credibility that millions of readers attach to the magazine — they suddenly attach to you. I'm not talking zillions of dollars here. I'm talking of a few thousand — and just one time. It's a small price to pay for credibility. You can get details about incredibly low costs for incredibly credible magazines by getting a free media kit from one of the companies your friendly search engine will disclose when you type in "remnant space."

GUERRILLA EXERCISE:

1. List the marketing vehicles you are now using to gain credibility for your company, including each medium in which you advertise.

2. List five other things you might do or say to enhance your credibility.

3. Make a timetable for doing those five things.

GUERRILLA ACTION STEPS:

1. Go through the magazines or newspapers in which you might advertise and determine which advertisers have the most credibility and why they have it.

2. Pay closer attention to the radio and television commercials you hear and see, determining which advertisers have the most credibility and why they have it.

3. Visit five websites, especially those of your competitors, and determine which have the most credibility and why they have it.

4. Make a new list of actions you can take right now to gain more credibility based upon what you've just learned. Take those actions. Putting your advertising on steroids is not a theory. It's a course of action.

CHAPTER 9

Economizing While Aggressively Advertising

ECONOMIZING WHILE AGGRESSIVELY ADVERTISING

When guerrilla marketers think of economizing, they don't necessarily think of trying to save money. What they do think of is <u>getting the absolute most from any money they've invested in advertising</u>. They realize there are really only two kinds of advertising — expensive and inexpensive — and they know that expensive advertising is the kind that doesn't cover the investment they've made, while inexpensive advertising pays rich rewards for their investment. Guerrillas know that economizing has nothing to do with cost; it has everything to do with results.

To be sure, guerrillas adopt a philosophy of frugality and thrift. They know well the difference between investing in something disposable such as paper and accounting services — and investing in something that's truly an investment, such as a telephone system or customer-tracking software — items they'd use on a daily basis. There's a big difference in these expenses, so you won't be surprised to learn that guerrillas rarely waste their time and effort on low cost disposable purchases, but are willing to expend the time and energy to enjoy a large savings on an expense that's really an investment in disguise.

A key to economizing is to think not in terms of purchasing, but in terms of acquiring. That means you open your mind to bartering, sharing, renting, modifying an existing item or borrowing it. It means possibly learning a few skills so that you can do rather than hire. Desktop publishing software enables you to save a ton of money usually paid to pros.

Guerrillas are also keenly aware of when it makes sense to hire a pro, knowing that amateur-looking advertising is an invitation to disaster. They might hire a highly-paid professional designer to give their marketing items a powerful visual format, and then use their own staff or themselves to continue generating advertising materials that follow this same format. They learn from any consultant they hire.

By understanding that economizing does not mean saving money, but investing it wisely, guerrillas test their investments on a small scale before plunging headlong into any kind of marketing. They have no fear of failure, providing the failures are small ones and knowing that even one success in ten tries means discovering a path to wealth and profitability.

They know in their hearts that money is not the key to happiness or success, but that enough of it enables them to have a key made. Real frugality is more about priorities and results than just saving money.

Of all the methods of wasting money and not economizing, the number one leader is failure to commit to a plan. Untold millions have been invested in advertising campaigns that had everything right about them except commitment on the part of the marketer. Guerrillas know that <u>it takes time for an investment to pay off and instant results are rarely part of the deal</u>.

Abandoning an advertising campaign before it has a chance to flourish squanders money in three ways. First, it means all prior investing in the campaign has been for naught. Second, it means new investing will be necessary to generate the share of mind that precedes a share of market. Third, it means creating new advertising materials all over again.

Small business owners have other ways to waste money as well. Many of them invest in research instead of doing it themselves. Others dare to commit to a campaign they haven't tested. Still others create advertising materials that must be updated regularly, rather than creating timeless advertising materials. When you say in a brochure that you've been in business five years, you must update that brochure next year. When you say you've been in business since 1996, that's always going to be the truth.

High on the list of ways that small business advertisers waste precious funds is their proclivity to invest in amusing advertising, funny advertising, and even uproarious advertising. Advertising has an obligation to put money in your coffers, not smiles on the faces of your prospects.

The most common method of economizing is also one of the most overlooked — advertising to existing customers. It costs one-sixth as much to sell an item to an existing customer than to sell that same item to a non-customer. The price of discovering and convincing likely customers is astronomical when compared with the price of doing the same with current customers.

Guerrillas avoid buying what they want and don't really need, don't fall prey to slick salespeople representing new and unproved advertising vehicles, avert bad decisions by not making quick decisions, and constantly ask themselves — "If I didn't need this yesterday, why do I need it today?"

Economic errors often made by entrepreneurs are failure to negotiate comparison shop or use the net for research. They don't know exactly where each of their dollars are going and don't know that the leaner their spending today, the fatter their cushion tomorrow. You'll constantly hear of new ways to get maximum bucks for your advertising investment. In fact, here are twelve more ways to accomplish that trick. But I hope you'll always keep in mind that the most important of the upcoming dozen tips for getting maximum bang for minimum bucks is to stick with one advertising campaign.

All advertisers who wish to put their advertising on steroids know that the primary advertising investment they make is not money, but time, energy and imagination. They secure their investments with patience, not in ample supply in these competitive times. They utilize this precious commodity to save money aggressively, as illustrated by these dozen ways they do it, beginning with the most important, yet most abused:

1. STICK WITH ONE MARKETING CAMPAIGN. Change the offer and price if you want, but don't change the media, the identity, or the visual format. It takes time for people to notice you, even more for them to trust you. Hang in there.

2. REALIZE THAT SMALL IS BEAUTIFUL. Allow your advertising to be masterminded by consultants, free-lancers, small ad agencies, using small ads run frequently and short commercials, too. Down goes the cost, up go the results.

3. USE A MEDIA-BUYING SERVICE. Ten years ago, the savvy strategy would be to have your own in-house agency. In advertising, that's the Dark Ages because media-buying services have better access to data and negotiating skills than you.

4. OBTAIN FREE RESEARCH BY DOING YOUR OWN AND GOING ONLINE. The currency of the 21st century is information, and there's more of it than ever. Create a customer questionnaire. Use the Net to compile mega-data.

5. USE REPRINTS OF PR AND ADS IN BROCHURES AND MAILINGS. Don't let a PR story pass without making zillions of reprints, framing them, blowing them up into posters, gaining their credibility for just pennies a copy.

6. CREATE TIMELESS BROCHURES. Never say in brochures "Our firm is 10 years old." Next year, you'll need a new brochure. Say, "Our firm was founded in 1991." That will always be true. Check brochures for timelessness.

7. FIND MULTIPLE USES FOR MATERIALS. Use the expensive photo taken for your advertisement in other places beyond the ad — in your brochures, as a sign, in a mailing, and use it over several years. This strengthens your visual identity and lets you amortize that expensive photo fee.

8. AVOID VAMPIRE MARKETING. That's the kind that sucks attention away from your main offer. It looks harmless as it harms your advertising thrust with humor, cleverness, special effects and snazzy production values. Sell biz is not show biz.

9. SPEND $1000 TO PRODUCE A TV SPOT. Yes, I know that in 2000, the average TV spot ran a cool $197,000 to produce, but it's possible, with the brute force of a power-packed idea, to make your point and spend under a grand. Happens daily.

10. WAIT FOR GANG RUNS. Full color has 57% more retention than black and white and increases inclination to buy by 41%. Gang runs give you full-color but not when you want it. You've gotta wait. Guerrillas do. Tell your printer you'll wait.

11. EXPERIMENT AND TEST. Be willing to take chances in your quest to find the perfect headline, the perfect ad medium, the perfect message. Only testing can give you the certainty you'll need to commit to your advertising program.

12. MARKET MORE TO CURRENT CUSTOMERS THAN TO PROSPECTS. As you know, it costs much less to market to an existing customer than it does to a non-customer. You

know where to find them, so sell to them and their friends.

If you put into practice any one, or especially all of these money-saving techniques, you'll begin to see how advertising works, why it works, why patience is such a valuable ally, and why so much advertising fails. Advertising is not costly, but advertising mistakes are very costly. Guerrillas have learned that the real key to saving money advertising is to waste no money. Putting your advertising on steroids has nothing to do with spending money and everything to do with not wasting it.

GUERRILLA EXERCISE:

1. Make a list of the purchases you plan to make and assess each one in terms of how canny an investment it is rather than how cheaply you can make the purchase.

2. Go through the twelve tips for saving money and put a checkmark next to each one of the twelve that you practice.

GUERRILLA ACTION STEPS:

1. Knowing the average U.S. business invested 4 percent of gross revenues in marketing during 2000, make a marketing budget for yourself for the coming year. Be sure to include activity for each month of the year and keep in mind that advertising is just one part of marketing.

2. Go back over the advertising that you have run and note the successes that you've had. Put into writing the factors that led to your success. Was it the headline, the offer, the graphics, the medium, the timing, the price, or some other factor? Guerrillas learn not only from their failures, but also from their successes.

CHAPTER 10

The Importance Of Your Identity

THE IMPORTANCE OF YOUR IDENTITY

If you're going to put your advertising on steroids, and that's the plan, be sure you don't ever try to cultivate an image. It can only get you into trouble. Every company, large and small, has a company personality. Guerrilla advertisers see to it that their personality is communicated properly.

Here's a common scenario from the world of advertising. Happens all the time. A group of people from a company decide to express their company's personality in all advertising materials, in sales presentations, at every opportunity. Misguided by traditions of the mid-20th century, the company advertising and management people decide to create an image for their company.

Sound the alarm! Call for the captain ashore!

These people are about to commit advertising mayhem and the fallout will fall over them. Advertisers who want to give an infusion of steroids to their advertising never ever create an image for their companies. They know that images are false. Images are phony. Image is even defined by the dictionary as "a facade."

A company decides upon some pie-in-the-sky image for their company, and then incorporates it, as they should, in every single one of their advertisements. Their target audience reads or views a message from this company, gets turned on by the image of the firm that's communicating, and decides to pay a visit to the company — or its website.

(At this point, it is fairly easy to hear the music from "Jaws" pounding away in the background. That's not your imagination. It's really sending those ominous tunes into your head.)

When folks show up at the company, they freeze up unconsciously. They see that these people are not exactly who they set themselves out to be. These people are someone else, someone not at all like the image they portrayed. On an inner, deeper level, where most purchase decisions takes place, the prospects feel a sense of distrust about the company. They feel as though they've been misrepresented to. Their confidence in the company begins to vaporize.

Why did this happen? Because the company relied upon the false idol of a just-pretend image instead of reality. What do guerrilla companies do to make their company personality known to their public? They communicate their identity.

They realize that an identity stems from truth and honesty, from reality. So they carefully avoid one "I-word" — Image, and head directly towards another "I-word" — Identity. They make certain: that all of their advertising materials communicate that identity, that it sings out clearly from everything their prospects and customers read and hear, that everyone in the organization understands that this is the company's identity. This is what their audience expects them to be. So what happens?

Their audience shows up and sees that these people are exactly who they expected. They are who they said they'd be; their company is what they said it was. As a result, prospects and customers feel an unconscious sense of trust in the company, a bonding. After all, they acted based upon what the company said, and the company was shunning a phony image while revealing an honest identity.

You'll find that much of the advertising process becomes easier once you've wrapped your mind around the idea of mining your honest identity instead of misinforming with some made-up image. Guerrillas are well aware that the highest form of public relations is human relations. They are able to blend warm relationships with sizzling profits.

No matter how good your advertising is, it can rarely bring customers back for more if they were disappointed with their first go-round with you. It cannot generate profits for you if your word-of-mouth advertising works against it. It can only get prospects to buy from you once. The rest is up to you — and up to your sense of humanity in marketing and advertising.

If you can't see the connection, perhaps marketing and advertising are not your strong points and you should become involved with something that does not involve human beings. Advertising very definitely does involve them. The more humanity they experience from your company, the more involved they'll be with you — and they'll prove it with repeat and referral business.

One guerrilla truism is that people like to buy from friends. Another is that it is crucial to make the human bond before you can make a lasting business bond. To avoid the depersonalization that has been an unpleasant side effect of the digital age and endemic within the business community, several marketing weapons may be employed to add humanity to your marketing and profits to your tiller.

On the retail level, it means using the weapons — and don't you dare underestimate their importance just because they're free — of a warm, sincere smile, clear eye contact, and whenever possible, using the person's name. Think of ways to make it possible. Realize that it feels human. It feels comfy. And that makes the person feel good. When the customer feels good, the customer connects you with that good feeling. That's why good feelings lead to good business.

Naturally, this should be your modus operandi during trade shows, whether you're an exhibitor or a browser. Parties on trade show evenings for key customers and prospects have been wise investments for the companies that want to intensify their human bonds. Guerrillas do not hesitate for a moment to play favorites.

The personality of your company, as heard on the telephone, can turn your customers on — or it can turn them off. A warm, friendly person answering the phone can lead to a warm, friendly relationship with your company. A cold, unfriendly person on the phone can make the caller feel intrusive, like an interruption of work rather than like the reason you exist.

If you absolutely must put the callers on hold, let them benefit from your on-hold advertising by listening to music in your identity and fascinating news about your company, especially about special offers and new products and services. Instead of resenting you, callers will appreciate you.

All contact time with customers should be oriented to the customer's needs, devoted to saving time for the customer. Even with your respect for the customer's time, there is still ample opportunity to strengthen the human bond by making the purchasing process as simple as possible. The idea is to be personable, to be streamlined, and to be easy to do business with.

Accept all credit cards. Provide partial payment plans. Offer overnight delivery. Encourage toll-free telephone ordering. Put up a content-rich website. Engage in sales training that includes pointers about human behavior and the immense power of a smile. Offer memory training to salespeople so they can connect names with faces. Be certain that anyone who will be in contact with your public is clear, pleasant, warm and a reflection of your company identity. Naturally, the best way to do this is when you are hiring. It is very difficult to train for lovability.

Your prospects are going to have to buy you and your reps before they buy what you and your reps are selling. Humanity that is sincerely added to a cold business situation warms up the transaction. It motivates the customer to be a source of repeat business and word-of-mouth referring.

Add humanity by asking questions, listening attentively to the answers, wanting to be of maximum service to the customer, providing free data in the form of brochures, newsletters, videos, and a website that responds instantly, the full gamut of guerrilla marketing weapons. Make warmth and humanity part of your written marketing plan. As basketball coach Phil Jackson says that his starting point in all relationships is compassion, make yours caring.

Most of the marketing weapons I've mentioned cost very little money. They are attitudes that serve to warm up your overall marketing. They make doing business with you more of a pleasure than a chore.

When your customers feel your caring, feel a sense of well-being because they're your customers, you have succeeded at one-on-one public relations. Who would ever think that a hallmark of the guerrilla is love? I hope you think it now.

GUERRILLA EXERCISE:

1. Put into writing a statement of your company's identity.

2. Examine every aspect of your marketing and advertising to make certain that it conveys your identity. If it doesn't change it.

GUERRILLA ACTION STEPS:

1. Look closely at the advertisements in the magazines and newspapers that you read. See if you can pick up on the advertiser's identity. Determine if the company is conveying a phony image or an honest identity.

2. Engage in serious conversation with key customers to determine your real identity. If your advertising is not communicating it, make the necessary changes.

3. Remember that Benjamin Franklin said that the two hardest things on earth are diamonds and knowing yourself. The more honestly you know yourself, the better equipped you'll be to communicate your honest identity.

CHAPTER 11

Putting Your Style And Your TV Spots On Steroids

PUTTING YOUR STYLE AND YOUR TV SPOTS ON STEROIDS

Because we're smack dab in the middle of The Information Age and because time is so darned important, guerrillas do not waste the time of the prospects and customers with gimmicks and pizzazz. Instead, they reward that time with beneficial information and solid content. The substance of their advertising is so lush, yet concise, that <u>substance is their style</u>.

Is your current advertising distinctive because of its style or substance? The ideal answer is both. With its style, it conveys your identity and captures the attention of your targeted audience. With its substance, it makes essential points and motivates that audience.

Well-informed advertisers see to it that both their style and substance are obvious but that their product or service always has the starring role in their advertising.

We've all had the experience of viewing a TV spot or reading an ad and wondering what the heck they were talking about, so you know what I'm getting at. Many websites are more confusing than they are enlightening.

In the early days of advertising, nobody needed special effects. When Harley Procter and his cousin, James Gamble, churned their soap too long and it floated, they came out and said Ivory is the soap that floats. Later, stressing its purity, they said it was 99 and 44/100ths percent pure. People knew exactly what they meant.

But now the creative revolution is upon us. In the name of creativity rather than the less glamorous but more accurate name of selling, billions of dollars are being wasted each year. That's a conservative estimate.

The creative rebels, award winners almost every one of them, are carried away by style, and in the melee, substance gets lost. Advertising is definitely not a shuck and jive show or an entertainment medium. Its purpose is selling and it should therefore be loaded with substance. You can be sure that the top salespeople in the world don't begin their presentations with a tap dance or a cartwheel. They succeed because of the style they use to provide substance, not because of the style itself.

The overriding concept in your advertising should be <u>to present substance and do it with style.</u> That means the emphasis is on the substance. The readers, viewers and website visitors remember the substance. Checks get written, credit cards used, and orders placed because of the substance.

Be on guard against the multitude of "creative" people that populate the advertising profession. Too many of them have been trained to create a gorgeous picture, a rhyming headline, or a flashing website when they should be trying to create an eye-popping upswing in your sales curve.

That sales curve is your responsibility. Remember, if "creative" ideas cost you more than they earn for you, something is wrong with the equation. The equation should read, "creativity equals profits."

Substance consists of both facts and opinions. It communicates both features and benefits. It is as specific as it can possibly be, as specific as 99 and 44/100th percent pure. And it effectively utilizes both words and pictures. What substance isn't, is <u>fun</u> — and you shouldn't try to make people think that is us unless you sell video games or bicycles.

It's <u>style</u> that's fun. Style makes your advertising enjoyable to read and hear. Or at least it makes your advertising digestible. Remember that your competition isn't Hollywood. It's that company that's been selling to your customers and attracting your prospects. Your competitors are people who don't have stars in their eyes, simply profits on their mind.

Given the relationship of substance to style, put your money on substance every time. But be aware that there are exceptions to this rule. If, for example, the very essence of your product or service is its style, you may want to convey that style as its primary benefit. The style is its substance.

But most businesses should <u>not even think</u> of selling with style at the expense of substance. Many have tried. Most have failed. Your task: stress your substance but do it with style.

One of the best places to demonstrate that style is with television commercials. Although it's true that the Internet will end up as the single most important way to reach your marketplace, that day is not yet with us. Until it is, television continues to reign supreme in the advertising spectrum.

Just as radio didn't disappear when TV entered our lives, TV won't disappear now that being online is rapidly becoming part of our lives. Yes, it's true that people are spending more time with their PCs and less time with their TVs and it's also true that the lines between them are blurring. But television deserves a place in the arsenal of a small business now more than ever.

The main reasons why this is true are:

- Television now allows you to target your audience more precisely than you could in the past. It lets you single out specific groups of people, such as business people, and it enables you to home in on selected neighborhoods in your community. These phenomena are due to the growth of cable TV.

- Television is now more affordable than it ever has been, in many cases lower in cost than radio. Direct response companies by the carload are discovering this and also discovering there is a 24-hour viewing audience out there with even lower rates and there are program-length infomercials that cost what regular one-minute spots used to cost. Again, we tip our hats to the cable industry for putting TV within everybody's reach.

■ This lesson will set you straight and tell you the truth about television use and production so that you avoid the multitude of mistakes made by non-guerrillas stumbling down the TV trail before you. You will end up understanding TV so clearly that it will be effective for you, though not from Day One. Guerrillas rarely expect reward before Day Ninety.

Is it really possible to learn about television in only one lesson? It is not only possible to do that but also possible to unlearn many fantasies you may have believing about television commercials. One such fantasy is that TV is supposed to entertain and amuse, make people laugh, be a work of art. Guerrillas don't fall for this joke. They know selling when they see selling. They know that advertising is a pretty fancy word that means selling and that selling has very little to do with entertaining and laughing.

Of the myriad of things you should know about television, I've limited my list here to only ten. There are one thousand ten things to know but these ten are the most important and every guerrilla knows them:

1. **Television is inexpensive**. The cost to run commercials is no more than $20 during prime time in most markets in the United States. The cost to produce a commercial, although $197,000 during 2000, should run you no more than $1000. You don't need Michael or Tiger or Dennis endorsing what you have to offer. And you're after sales, not Emmys.

2. **Television is a visual medium.** Don't think of it as a radio spot with pictures. Think of it as a visual story with a beginning, a middle and an end. Because over 70 percent of us mute the commercials with our remote zappers, if you're not telling your story and saying your name visually, you're not telling your story or saying your name at all.

3. **Television is powered by an idea.** Forget the special effects, music, staging and lighting. First think of the idea. That's what makes a commercial successful — a strong offer, a visual expression of a good idea. Once you have the idea, everything else will fall into place. Without the idea, your commercial has hardly any chance of success.

4. **Television is made fascinating by special effects.** Many people get carried away at their opportunities to be like Steven Spielberg and fall prey to gizmos and gimmicks. Use special effects to highlight your idea, to focus on your idea, to further your idea and then you'll see why they're so special. Otherwise, they act like vampires, sucking attention away from your offer with their dazzle.

5. **Television doesn't cost as little as you think.** Here I am telling you right off the bat that TV is inexpensive and here I am one minute later telling you that it's not so inexpensive. The spots are inexpensive. The production can be inexpensive. But you've got to run several spots every day, several days

a week, three weeks out of four, and for a minimum of three months — unless you're making a direct response offer — before you see any glimmerings that TV is about to do the job for you. If you're looking for instant gratification, look somewhere other than the tube.

6. **Television is made better if you operate from a script.** You need not waste your precious money having somebody produce a storyboard for you because you don't need one. But you do need a script that tells the exact visuals and the exact sounds that will go on for 30 seconds.

7. **Television production costs are lower when you pre-produce with care.** The way guerrillas cut 196,000 ugly dollars from their TV production costs is by have pre-production meetings where all production details are handled. These are followed by rehearsals for the talent and the technicians. There should be zero surprises on the day of the TV shooting.

8. **Television production costs are lowered still if you produce your sound track first.** After you've got it, you can shoot footage to match the amount of time the words and music take. Shooting sound and picture at the same time means that if a plane flies overhead or a truck drives by, you've got to re-shoot. Do your sound first, using professionals, then shoot the visuals.

9. **Television's greatest strength is its ability to demonstrate.** As newspapers give the news and magazines involve readers, as

radio provides intimacy and direct response adds urgency, television's power is the way it can demonstrate. It can show before and after, with a shot of the product in use during the middle. It can hit left and right-brained people. It can combine all the art forms into a masterful blending of show and sell.

10. **Television is still the undisputed heavyweight champion of marketing**. I love online marketing so much that I'm nearly bursting with enthusiasm for it. I know it's gonna make every other medium stronger and more effective. And I know it's not a matter of if, but a matter of when you go online. Until then and after then, you'll find that television can talk directly to your specific target audience, that it will cost you much less than you figured, and that if you've got the patience to commit to a TV campaign, you're going to be delighted at how it rewards your patience.

A final word: Just as being online doesn't mean beans unless it's part of a well-crafted marketing program, being on television is also no guarantee of profitability unless it is part of a program and supported with other media.

Never forget that somebody once defined a TV commercial as "a dream interrupter." I look forward to your commercials interrupting my dreams.

GUERRILLA EXERCISE:

1. Review your past and planned advertising to determine whether you've been focusing on substance or style. Do what you must to adjust all future advertising to focus on both.

2. Watch television with an eagle eye towards spotting the basic idea of the commercial. You'll probably be appalled at the paucity of ideas. Meaning: there's a superb arena out there just waiting for guerrillas who understand the immense power of television.

GUERRILLA ACTION STEPS:

1. Create a thirty-second TV spot for your company. On the left side of the page, put the visuals you wish to show. On the right side, put the words. Figure that you can use a maximum of 70 words — and remember that most people will view your spot with the sound off. So be sure to tell your story visually.

2. Select the channels and TV shows most likely to be viewed by your target audience. Remember that cable TV is always less expensive than network TV. So favor the economy of running your commercials on one of the many cable channels.

CHAPTER 12

Discovering Memes — The Newest Secret In Advertising

DISCOVERING MEMES — THE NEWEST SECRET IN ADVERTISING

The prehistoric man, Uba, spent all day in the rain trying to catch a fish because his family was very hungry and in dire need of food. But he was unable to grab a fish from the stream even though he occasionally got his hands on one. Frustrated and weak from hunger, he just couldn't grab any fish firmly enough because it would slither from his hands and return to the stream. Worse yet, the light rain turned to a heavy rain and Uba was forced to seek shelter in a nearby cave.

Entering it, when his eyes became accustomed to the dark, he noticed a series of paintings in the cave. One depicted a deer. Another represented a godlike figure. But it was the third that captured his attention. There on the cave wall, was a simple drawing — a stick figure of a man holding a long stick. At the end of the stick, a fish was impaled. Suddenly, Uba got the idea! Within an hour, he returned to his family carrying five fish, all of which he had caught with a stick that had one end sharpened.

Uba's family was saved by a meme. A meme is a self-explanatory symbol, using words, action, sounds, or in this case, pictures, that communicate an entire idea. Uba may have discovered the first meme in history.

Since Uba's time, there have been many more memes. In fact, as much as you used to see the word "Internet," during the nineties, that's about as many times as you'll see the word "memes" during the aughts.

Memes in advertising are a whole new idea. Some have existed, but those were created long before the concept of memes was known. The word meme, though coined in 1976 by Oxford biologist Richard Dawkins in his book, "The Selfish Gene," has been the architect of human behavior since the beginning of time. The wheel was major improvement in transportation and conveyance, and was also a meme because it was a self-explanatory symbol representing a complete idea.

There are three things you should know about memes:

1.   It's the lowest common denominator of an idea, a basic unit of communication.

2.   It has the ability to alter human behavior.

3.   It is energized with emotion.

In guerrilla advertising, a meme's purpose is profiting, selling, motivating, and communicating instantly how your product or service improves lives. It can do this with words (Lean Cuisine), pictures (Marlboro cowboy), sounds (from the valley of the jolly ho ho ho, Green Giant), actions (Clydesdales pulling Budweiser wagon), or imagery (Burger-King's flame-broiled image).

For guerrillas, a meme is a concept that has been so simplified that anybody can understand it instantly and easily. Within two seconds you must convey who you are, why someone should buy from you instead of a competitor, trigger an emotional response and generate a desire.

To put you even more on my wavelength, consider many of the other memes we have learned to know and possibly even love:

Healthy Choice

Be Direct — Dell

Intel inside

Got milk?

Capitalist Tool — Forbes

Panasonic — just slightly ahead of our time

Where do you want to go today?

America Online

Drivers wanted — VW

I'm going to Disneyland!

UPS — moving at the speed of business

M&Ms melt in your mouth, not in your hands

SlimFast

Weight Watchers

NBC — must-see TV

A diamond is forever

Toys R Us

Staples — yeah, we've got what you want

Foot Joy

V for victory

Gatorade poured on winning coach

Things go better with Coke

7-Up —-The uncola

I want my MTV!

The Mall of America

Snap, crackle and pop

Keep in mind that in advertising, a meme is an idea or concept that has been refined, distilled, stripped downs to its bare essentials, and then super-simplified in such a way that anybody can grasp its meaning instantly and effortlessly.

Try to imagine a motorist speeding down a highway, just entering a curve. All of a sudden, a billboard comes into view. It shows a mutilated child, an ambulance, paramedics, flashing lights, weeping parents and a grim police officer. The billboard copy: Speed kills.

The combined effect of the photo and copy constitutes a meme that instantly, effortlessly and lucidly transmits an entire complex message into a human mind in a single involuntary glance. If you saw it while driving, there is little doubt that you would cut your speed without even thinking about it on a rational level.

From Geoff Ayling's "Rapid Response Advertising," (Business and Professional Publishing, 1998, Warriewood, Australia, we learn that memes have an enormous impact on our lives. They invade our minds without either our knowledge or our permission, and initiate a chain reaction. They create an involuntary shift in perception, which in turn creates a shift in attitude, which creates a shift in behavior — and that is the ultimate goal of all marketing.

With so much advertising, both online and offline, assailing our senses, it's more important now than ever to create a meme for your own company. I didn't say it was easy, but I am saying it is mandatory if you're to stand out in an ever-competitive crowd — a crowd that relishes its time more than ever. Don't be like Uba and wait till you're all wet and hungry.

As important as it is for you to know about memes, it's equally important that you remember that there are at least 100 weapons of marketing and that advertising is only one of them. Just because you're advertising with vigor, doesn't mean you're marketing with vigor. Advertising is only part of the puzzle — perhaps the biggest and costliest part, but still — only part. Even when you do it right, don't expect instant results.

How long do you have to wait to see the results you want? Whatever you do, don't hold your breath while waiting for your advertising to take affect. Instead, hold your horses because it's not gonna happen instantly.

To determine how long it takes for a prospect to become a customer first look into the chemistry of prospects. Prospects are like you, except that they're probably doing business with one of your competitors. Fortunately for you, that competitor most likely doesn't know the full meaning of follow-up, with the result that most customers feel ignored after the sale.

These are among your hottest prospects. They already do business with a company such as yours and may be disenchanted because they've been left alone after making their purchase. That's why guerrillas identify their best prospects and then begin the courtship process. <u>It is a courtship and it is a process</u>. Armed with that insight, you can transform them into customers.

Most business owners contact prospects once or twice, and if they don't show an interest, the business owners move on to greener territories, on to the non-existent Land of Instant Gratification. Guerrillas continue romancing those they are courting. Eventually, those prospects feel so cared for, so important, so attended to, that they switch over and begin to patronize the guerrilla who never stops courting.

How long does it take until this happen? Try seven years on for size. That's the outside. It could happen in a month, even a week or less if the prospects are in the market right now and neglected by their former supplier. But it probably won't happen soon and it most assuredly won't happen if you ignore them after contacting them once or twice.

Remember that prospects have minds that are more open than you think. Allegiances that are lost every day, allegiances gained every day. The guerrilla marketers don't lose them because they recognize the slow motion process of gaining them. When they speak to prospects, whether in person or through one of the venues of advertising, they do not talk about their businesses or their industries. They talk about the prospects themselves — which is the topic most on the mind of prospects and one that ceaselessly interests them. When guerrillas can talk about the problems facing prospects, they gain even more attention.

And when they talk about solutions to these problems, they still see things from the prospects' points of view and talk from that mindset. As weeds are flowers whose beauty has not yet been discovered, prospects are customers who have not yet realized all that you can offer them.

Give them time. Give them information. Give them attention. While you're waiting, walk a mile in their shoes so you can be better prepared to talk to them about how their feet feel.

People patronize the businesses they do for an enormously wide variety of reasons. Often, it's location, though the Internet is changing that in a hurry. Frequently, it is mere habit. Guerrillas know in their bones that the prime reason is the buyers have confidence in the sellers. That is closely followed by the quality of the offering. And next comes service — which guerrillas know should be defined as "anything the customer wants it to be." After service comes selection — and again the Internet rears up as a contender for business because of the staggering breadth of its selection. And fifth comes price. To some people, fewer than 20 percent, price is the number one criterion. But those attracted by price make the most disloyal customers because they're easily wooed away by somebody offering a still lower price. <u>Guerrillas build their businesses on loyal customers.</u> Possessed with that insight, they do all in their power to maintain loyalty.

They may do it with frequent-buyer programs. They may do it with special events centered around customers. They may do it with fervent follow-up, with their newsletter, with little freebies for their customers. But most of them do it by recognizing the customer and using his or her name, by talking about personal things before getting down to business, by listening very carefully and sincerely to what their customers are saying. Listening is considered one of the most crucial parts of follow-up. It's no surprise that people patronize businesses that listen to them.

Many advertisers create their advertising under the ridiculous assumption that prospects are asking "Who are you? What is your product or service? When are you open? Where are you located?" The only real question in the prospect's mind is "Why should I care?"

Here's what they're thinking: It's not "tell me a story about you." Instead, it's "tell me a story about me." Tell me how you can save my time, increase my income, reduce my stress, bring more love into my life, cause people to think highly of me." If you can't talk to them about those things, leave those prospects alone because you're wasting their time and your money.

Another insight possessed by guerrillas is that people patronize businesses that can offer things to change their lives for the good. Sometimes these are huge things, such as cars and computers. But usually they're not. After all, how much can a new shirt or a new paper stock for stationery change a life? Not much, but you've still got to be thinking in those terms.

Keep in mind that people are attracted to businesses that have established credibility. You get it with superb advertising and commitment to a plan.

Advertising continues to be a blend of art, science, business and patience. It works. But it rarely works instantly. That's why the most crucial ingredient in the blend called marketing is your own patience.

GUERRILLA EXERCISE:

1. Keep a running list of how many memes you see in advertising. Even if you keep meticulous records for a week, you'll see very few — indicating that the competition isn't yet aware of this powerful new secret in advertising.

2. Make a list of the benefits that you offer and try to express each one visually. This is the first step in creating a meme for your company.

GUERRILLA ACTION STEPS:

1. Make a list of all the marketing weapons that you use now, remembering that advertising is only one of them.

2. Eliminate from that list the marketing weapons that don't seem to be giving you a healthy return on your investment. Double up on those which give you the kind of return you want.

NOTES:

NOTES: —————————————

NOTES:

NOTES:

NOTES:

NOTES:

GET THE COMPLETE GUERRILLA ARSENAL!

Guerrilla Marketing for the New Millennium

A complete reworking of Jay Conrad Levinson's guerrilla "manifesto". Learn to think and market like a guerrilla and crush your competitors.

ISBN: 1-933596-07-4   Paperback
ISBN: 1-933596-08-2   eBook
ISBN: 1-933596-09-0   CD Audio

Guerrilla Marketing: Put Your Advertising on Steroids

Jay Conrad Levinson takes the proven concepts of the world's most successful companies, and synthesized them into a new type of marketing that any business can use to make mega-profits. This is Barely Legal... But You Can Still Get Away With It!

ISBN: 1-933596-13-9   Paperback
ISBN: 1-933596-14-7   eBook
ISBN: 1-933596-15-5   CD Audio

Guerrilla Copywriting

60 Profitable Tips in 60 Enlightening Minutes. Jay Conrad Levinson and David Garfinkel join forces to give small business owners, executives and marketing professionals 60 essential tactics, strategies and concepts for producing highly effective marketing messages.

ISBN: 1-933596-20-1   CD Audio

Guerrilla Marketing During Tough Times

Find Out Why Your Business Is Slowing Down. Jay Conrad Levinson shows you exactly why your business is slowing down in tough economic times and exactly what you can do about it.

ISBN: 1-933596-10-4   Paperback
ISBN: 1-933596-11-2   eBook
ISBN: 1-933596-12-0   CD Audio

Guerrilla Marketing 101: Lessons From The Father Of Guerrilla Marketing — DVD/Workbook Bundle

This 4-Volume set contains over 5 hours of business-building secrets personally presented by Jay Conrad Levinson, Father of the Worldwide Guerrilla Marketing Revolution.

ISBN: 1-933596-16-3   Bundle
ISBN: 1-933596-17-1   DVD
ISBN: 1-933596-18-X   Workbook

Guerrilla Marketing 101: Lessons From The Father Of Guerrilla Marketing — Bootlegged

Over 4 hours of Bootlegged, CD Quality Audio, from the GM 101 Set. Never before revealed tactics and insights from the Father of Guerrilla Marketing.

ISBN: 1-933596-30-9   CD Audio

These items are available through bookstores or directly through Morgan James Publishing at http://www.MorganJamesPublishing.com.

GET YOUR FREE GIFT!

Until now, no marketing association in existence could make a business bulletproof. But once again, Jay Conrad Levinson, the most respected marketer in the world, has broken new ground. The Guerrilla Marketing Association is quite literally a blueprint for business immortality.

Receive a **two-month FREE trial membership** in the Guerrilla Marketing Association where Guerrilla Marketing coaches and leading business experts answer your business questions online and during exclusive weekly telephone chats. This $99 value is your gift for investing in *Guerrilla Marketing: Put Your Advertising On Steroids!*

Join right now before your competition does
at http://www.Morgan-James.com/gma.

To purchase additional Guerrilla Marketing products by Jay Conrad Levinson, visit the Morgan James Publishing Bookstore at http://www.MorganJamesPublishing.com.

Printed in the USA
CPSIA information can be obtained
at www.ICGtesting.com
JSHW082212140824
68134JS00014B/587